Confessions

Sway Dodson

BookLeaf
Publishing

India | USA | UK

Presentation by *BookLeaf Publishing*

Web: www.bookleafpub.com

E-mail: info@bookleafpub.com

ISBN: 9789357444200

First edition 2022

DEDICATION

To everyone wondering if that one poem is
about you.

I'd tell you that it's not,

But that would be a lie :)

(thanks for the inspiration)

Why I Write

Why do you write?

That's a terrible question.
Here's a better one:

Why do you breathe?
To sustain your body,
to keep yourself alive,
because it's an instinct.

Why do I write?
To sustain my mind,
to keep my soul alive,
because it's an instinct.

Why do I write?

I write to empty my head of thoughts.
I treat poetry like a diary,
word vomit filling the page.

I write to cope with the feelings
that often overtake me.
The feelings that I cannot describe
with spoken words.

I write to feel calm.
When I see the words on the page,
I get this feeling that's like no other.

I write to immortalize the moments
that only you and I know.

I write for myself.
My words are my secrets,
a confession of the keyboard.

Love Note #2

I am a hopeless romantic.

I know,
That's what everyone says.

I am so in love with the idea of being in love
I'm scared it won't feel as good as it does in my
fantasies.

I want all the cute
romantic stuff,
the things that new couples do together.

I want someone to look at me
with admiration and love in their eyes,
and with that one look,
you know that they care about you so much.

I want to talk for hours and hours and hours
I want to talk for so long
that our voices become hoarse from talking and
laughing.

I want to stay up late with someone
not keeping track of the time

and fall asleep in their arms.

I want to have makeout sessions that are just that
I never got to do that when I was fifteen.

I want my cheeks to hurt from smiling
because I cannot get this person out of my head.

I want to know someone so well
and for them to know me
that we can ace a couple's trivia game.

I want someone to come home to
after a long day of work
to find that they have cooked my favorite meal.

I want someone to love me
even when I look and feel my worst.
I want them to cuddle me
and take all my troubles away.

I want someone who's spontaneous
who will book a vacation without working out
all the details.

I want someone who will
bring me flowers for special occasions,
and for ordinary days.

I want all of this
and more.

I want to be so in love with someone
that they're all I think about.

Repeat

When we part,
I'm convinced I'm hypnotic,
that I made you up.

You came from my wildest dreams.
You're hard to believe.

It takes a while to sink in,
the fact that you're real.

It's impossible,
it's unbelievable,
It's true.

When your name appears on my phone,
it doesn't matter what you've said.
Whether you sent me a funny video,
or you're sharing your feelings,
My heart races,
the butterflies swirl.

When we're together,
I feel complete,
I feel like you were always meant to be beside
me.

I feel
excitement
You know how to make me smile,
you know how to
take my words away.

When your lips meet mine
I feel passion,
warmth.

When your hands touch my skin
my nerves tingle,
like fireworks.
I never thought those could be real.

You leave me craving,

lingering in my head,

until next time.

Repeat

Nights Like These

Nights like these are my favorite

Nights where
The silence around me is comforting,
the air outside is freezing,
and I'm the only person awake

On nights like these
I feel free,
like the dark of the night will empower me,
allow me to see things
that disappear with the moon

Nights like these
give order to my thoughts,
bring energy in my veins.
I feel alive

Nights like tonight,
the perfection of it all,
makes me think of you

What it would be like to fall asleep
with my head on your chest,
the rhythmic beat of your heart

a lullaby

What would it be like
to wake up in your arms,
for your eyes to be the first thing I see

I don't think I'd ever look at these nights
the same again.
These nights could never live up to that

So come join me
on a night like this

rewind resend reset

Please

Somebody
tell me

Where

can I find
the button
in my
head

That will make
this
go
away

Please
let
me

rewind resend reset

Can we

reset?

Can we go
back?

Back to
yesterday?

the battle
in my head
rages

I don't know
if I
want to

Why didn't
you
speak up?

That's all
I
wanted

I'm not mad
yes
I promise

I'm just

thinking

Rewind.

Resend.

Reset.

Screwed Up

I screwed up,
again

It always blows up.
It can never be
just
a conversation

You make me feel
like I'm
nothing.

Not worth the time,
or energy.

You lace your words with venom
Biting,
Lashing,
Burning

I don't know
what you want me
to say,

you don't like it

either way.

The music helps
drown it out,

but even the music
can't keep out
the thoughts,

the worry,
doubts,
insecurities.

All the things
you planted
inside my head

Go ahead,
keep going,
screw me up some more.

Confession

The words were on the tip of my tongue
I almost let them loose
those three loaded words

Alone,
those words mean separate things

I
me
the person who notices every flaw about myself
every insecurity, every doubt

Love
the concept that everyone is chasing
the feelings that makes us all stupid

You
my favorite person
the one I can't stand to be away from

Together, those words mean something
that should only be shared
if you truly mean it
they should only be returned
when you truly mean it

I love you
I truly mean that
with my entire soul

The way you look at me
I've only seen that kind of look on TV
when the guy is so addicted to the girl
you can see it in his eyes
It's a look of adoration
it's the look of pure happiness
it radiates from him, the guy on TV
And it radiates from you

I wanted to say it that day
when we pulled back from a hug
the look on your face
Pure adoration
for me, of all people
The words were right there
I'm so in love with you
I bit my lip to hold them back

What? You asked
What are you thinking?

Nothing, I replied

Tell me, you said, smiling

I'm just so happy, I said
And that's true
I am so happy with you

But that's not what I wanted to say
in that moment

Realizations

I'll remember tonight being pivotal.
Pivotal,
for me

Call me crazy,
say it's too soon

But
I realized something that night.
it came on suddenly,
the feeling rushed over me,
it was overwhelming

I realized something.
Something
I hadn't thought of before

Something
I was hesitant to think

I realized

I don't want this life
without you,

I can't imagine growing up
with someone else,

I don't want to reach milestones
without you by my side,

I realized

I'd rather have nobody,
if you're not here

I'd sooner tackle the hardships alone
then have another hand in mine.

I realized

You're all I'll ever need.

You're everything to me.

I realized

I'm falling in love with you.

Manipulation

No, not today.
My brain's too fuzzy.

You've done this before

"Toxic,"
You say.
but that word is better suited
for you

I've always given more
tried more,
loved more.

That ends tonight

Words spilled over.
I meant all of them.

"Trust issues,"
Go ahead,
shift the blame

Assumptions,

conclusions.

Control.
That's what this is for you

Explosion.

Manipulation.

Deep Truths, Bared With Experimental Affection

I might have been the first one to break his heart
the boy with the ice-cube-colored eyes
We both had a crush on each other for a while
And for a while, we could have been good
together
but people change. Kids change rapidly.
I changed.
I don't remember if you did
You gave me an expensive pair of earrings for
Christmas
you didn't speak in that moment
you handed me the box and walked away
I wondered if your mother bought them for you
with me in mind
I felt strange in that moment
I didn't want those earrings from you
I don't remember how things ended
but it was shortly after that

I have a confession:

You were never special enough for me

You were the first to break my heart
at least, that's what I thought in the moment
I don't remember how our "relationship" began
or if you can even call it that
We talked in class
and over email
We held hands on the way to the bus
your hand was way too sweaty
you never tried to kiss me
Looking back
I don't remember if you were funny
or sweet
I was so caught up in the idea of a boyfriend
I looked past your immaturity
The first time we broke up
you sent a friend over to tell me
I remember thinking that you were a coward
why hadn't you told me yourself
Over the summer, we got back together
we were up late sending emails to each other
I remember your message
I love you
I freaked out and dumped you for good that
night
I remember thinking

Who the hell says I love you at twelve years
old?
You told me we would date in high school
we never did and I'm glad for it
And just like the boy before you
there was nothing extraordinary about you

I have a confession:
You were never man enough to handle me

You and I were very different people
You were a football player. You were popular
everyone knew who you were
I was a loner
I had blue hair at one point that year
We had English 3 together
an honors class
at first look, I was surprised you took that class
We were put into the same group
to work on a project spanning the entire
semester
I quickly realized you weren't just a dumb jock
you were actually smart
and funny
You were always nice to me when we worked
together
I talked about you to my friends
I had a major crush on you

I fantasized about asking you out
but I waited too long
On the last day of school,
I saw you with another girl
you probably would have turned me down
anyway

I have a confession:
The person I am now is way too good for you

You had kind eyes
you laughed at my nerdy jokes
and made some nerdy jokes of your own
Your humor was what drew me to you
Looking back
I think that was the only reason I liked you
I flirted with you a bit in class
you didn't notice
I should have taken that hint
I made up a short survey to ask you
I claimed it was for my statistics class
You didn't know that I had taken statistics the
previous year
my questions were ordinary
How old are you
What grade are you in
Do you drive
I approached you walking in the hallway

your friend was walking with you
I asked you the questions
I couldn't get to my last one though
Would you like to go out with me sometime
For two reasons
One, anxiety was clawing up my throat the
entire time
I could feel my heartbeat in my head
Two, your friend never left your side
I didn't want to be rejected in front of someone
else
and I didn't want you to say yes in front of
someone else

I have a confession:
I never regretted not being able to ask that
question

You messaged me on Instagram
I knew you from class, but that was it
You were having a hard time
I didn't empathize with you though
You told me that you wanted more with your
best friend
but she didn't
You told me you were depressed
I kept thinking

that you were dramatic and overreacting
that you were desperate for attention
Just take the hint
You messaged me everyday, nonstop
I would try to ease your worries and tell you it
would get better
but you always had an excuse
You asked me invasive questions
I know now that I shouldn't have answered
You became increasingly irritating
I thought you saw me as a sort-of therapist
but I quickly realized you had developed a crush
on me
I pretended like I didn't notice
I was only friendly to you, nothing more
Some might say I strung you along
In some ways, I did. I should have shut you
down sooner
You became increasingly creepy
you asked my best friend for a way to ask me
out
she told you that I didn't like you
You persisted
Just take the hint
At this point, I was protecting myself against
you
I ignored all of your messages
I had my friends in class sit in the desks
surrounding me

You persisted still
I blocked your number and your Instagram
account
Did you finally get the hint

I have a confession:
I've wondered if your behavior escalated to you
hurting someone

I saw you one afternoon at the grocery store
four years later
Your football days were long gone
you looked good
I felt like I was walking in slow-motion when I
saw you
instantly, I felt like I was fifteen again
shy, wide-eyed, awkward
It didn't help that I looked like a hot mess
a messy bun, t-shirt, athletic shorts, and flip
flops
I was snacking while I shopped
You were on my mind the entire night
I asked my best friend if I should message you
Go for it, girl
I sent the message past midnight
It was a bit flirty, but not overly so
I went to bed feeling proud of myself that I shot
my shot

You responded the next morning
Hope everything is going well for you
that's when I knew you weren't interested
Even so, I messaged back
How are you
you told me you were training to become a
firefighter
I asked if you had always wanted to do that
Yes ma'am
I remember feeling shocked by that message
then laughing
I left him on read and deleted our messages
I felt like I had failed at flirting
I knew, rationally, that there were many other
factors at play there
but I was down for a couple days after that
I was too caught up in a fifteen-year-old's
fantasy
I know now how ridiculous this all was

I have a confession:
I realize now you would have treated me badly

I noticed you on the first day of class
you were really cute
Our professor said your name
I looked you up online a couple weeks later and
followed you

I showed your account to my mom and looked at
the same pictures for weeks
I wanted to talk to you
I had planned to sit next to you in class one day
but I was running late
when I got there, someone else was sitting next
to you
I remember driving out of the parking lot one
day
you were walking to your car
my windows were rolled down
we might have made eye contact; I don't
remember
I quickly looked away and continued driving
The next week, our professor let us out of class
early
I thought about asking you out, right then and
there
but I wanted to talk to you before that
The idea of you faded in my head
I had decided to let fate take the wheel
If it's meant to be, it will be
One day, I posted something about writer's
block to my Instagram story
you replied
We stayed up until nearly 2 AM that night
talking
you asked me if I wanted to hang out that
weekend

Offered to take me to Frankie's
I said yes
We agreed to meet up for ice cream the day
before Frankie's
I've spent the past seven weeks with you
I can't get you out of my head
I could list all the things I like about you
You're so damn cute
at the same time you're hot
You're actually funny
the sound of your laughter gives me life
You tease me after you kiss me
you hold my hand while you're driving
You listen to the music I like
You never leave me on read
You ask me about things I know you have no
interest in
You give me your jackets to wear
You're not afraid to be authentic
you encourage me to do whatever I want

You're absolutely perfect

I could also list the ways you're different from
the others
You're special, unlike him
You're not a coward like him
You're much more than funny, unlike him
You're not creepy like him

You show that you care about me, unlike him

I have a confession:
I'm so in love with you

Three

The hardest part of losing someone
is not the day they leave,
or the day of the funeral,
it's not even the grief
The hardest part of losing someone
Is realizing all the things they will miss
and realizing all the things
I should have done differently

My grandmothers
didn't see me graduate high school,
or turn eighteen
I couldn't call them
the morning I started college,
or when my professor scolded me in class
They'll never see me graduate college
They will never meet my boyfriend
I won't get to call them
when he pisses me off
I won't get to call them
if I ever make the New York Times bestselling
list
They'll never
go wedding dress shopping with me
They'll never smile at me with tears in their eyes

as I walk down the aisle in a poofy white gown
My grandmothers
will never get to hold my children,
or give me parenting advice,
or have us over for the weekend
I have to face these milestones
without them

I regret now
not calling them more
I regret
not making time for them
They were always so supportive of my art
I should have returned the affection
I should have visited them more
I miss you

All I'm left with
is a deadbeat grandfather,
whom I haven't thought about in months,
and who couldn't care less about me.

Sometimes I wish it had been you.

Can you come over?

Can you come over?
I don't feel good
mentally
or
physically

Can you come over
and hold me while I sleep?

stroke my hair
cuddle me
envelop me in your scent
run your fingers up and down my spine
kiss my forehead

Can you come over
and hold me if I need to cry?

be patient with me
as I struggle to find words
explaining how I'm feeling

Can you come over
and spend the night?

hold me all night long
I'll feel your love in your arms
and I'll wake up to breakfast already done

This is all I want from you
this is all I'll ever ask of you

If I ask you
Would you come?

I'm on my way
I'll see you in 30

BLURRY

What is this?
forgetfulness--
distractions--
impulses--

My head feels blurry--too full

I can't focus
But--
why?

Fluttering ideas
Gone as soon as they come

Motivation--
what's that?

I feel like I have no control
My mind
Constantly racing--
running laps

I can't catch up with my words--
just out of my grasp

Am I in control?

Please--
slow down

Please--
give me my words back

Please--
return my focus

Where's the girl I know
focused--
attentive--
responsible--

She's gone wherever the words are

I don't make sense anymore

Do I feel better now?

Is this the rest of me--
scattered
tempered
problematic

Is this the rest of my life--
blurry

muddled
unfocused

Just tell me it gets better--
too fast
too fuzzy
too much

Tell me I'll learn--
how to breathe
how to feel
how to see

Just tell me--
Anything--

Is this the way it will always be?

The Diner

It was the summer of '96
Everyone was drunk on love,
or just in love
with the idea of love

I had goals
I wanted a career,
and I wanted to go to college

The Diner was my way out
Plain, unassuming,
black-topped barstools,
and red, cracking booths,
a black-and-white checkered floor

Laura,
my first customer
She was young,
and pregnant
Her dark hair fell around her ghostly face
She wore expensive clothes,
and expensive jewelry,
the kind that shines
even in bad lighting
A huge engagement ring adorned her tiny hand

She had sad eyes,
haunted eyes
She wore a defeated expression

She ordered a decaf coffee
and a slice of blueberry pie

"Are you alright?"

Her fiance had cheated on her
I abandoned my other tables to sit with her
At any other restaurant, I would have been fired
for that,
but The Diner was a homely place
It had something for everyone

When she went home,
she left her engagement ring for me
as a tip
She wrote me a note with two words and her
phone number
Thank you

I sold the ring and bought a car,
which I drove to see her the next day
and every other day after that
We were inseparable
she named me godmother of her son

I still see her every now and then
she's my best friend

Daniel,
my most memorable customer
He came in an hour before closing
he wore military clothes
I wasn't sure what branch

"Are you ready to order?"
He asked me what my favorite meal was
I told him that I liked the grilled cheese combo
that's what he ordered
He was polite and respectful

He followed me outside during my smoke break
he told me he'd be here
for the next two weeks
and that was it
He asked me out
I said yes
He kissed me before my cigarette was out

It was the best two weeks of my life
We broke into the Y
and went skinny dipping
We fell asleep in the bed of his truck
after shooting fireworks
We spent an entire day at the arcades

He was unlike any other man I'd ever met
sensitive
tender
I would not have pegged him
for a military guy

I really loved him
I think he loved me, too
But we never exchanged that promise

I watched his plane take off
when it was time for him to go
I was devastated
I cried at the airport
He was the first man I ever loved
He left a scar on my heart
that never healed

June,
my most interesting customer
She drove up to The Diner
In a '75 Volkswagen van
I could tell it was blue at one point,
but it was so sunbleached and chipped,
that it appeared to be white

I remember what she was wearing
white platform boots,

a patchwork dress
with thirty different patterns,
a jean jacket
with jeweled tassels covering the back
The tassels were obscured
by her long, wheat-colored hair

She came right up to the counter
while I was totaling a bill
She ordered a strawberry milkshake to-go
I complimented her style
she told me I was beautiful
We flirted while my coworker mixed her shake
She left with a wink,
but came back later that night
She picked me up in the van
we drove to an abandoned parking lot
We got high listening to '70s music
and kissed
until my shift the next morning
I never saw her again

She helped me heal a bit
after Daniel left
I never thanked her for that

Corey was my last customer
He walked into The Diner with three other guys
they were all wearing black and red leather

he wore eyeliner
His curls fell in front of his eyes
when I first saw him

The guys with him chose a booth
but Corey walked up to the counter
He smiled at me
the kind of smile that makes you stop
and lose all the words in your head
We had an instant connection

He was in a band
they were on their first tour
They ordered just about everything on the menu
and didn't sit in my section,
but I went out of my way to check on them
Corey was captivating
I couldn't keep my eyes off of him
The feeling was mutual

When they were leaving,
I yelled for them to wait
I tossed my apron and name tag to a manager
and I finished the tour with them

When we reached Las Vegas,
Corey and I got a little drunk
we wrote a song together
I was so in love

at that moment
We went into town
and got married

Our song
became the band's number one hit
Corey sang it to me
last week
as we celebrated our anniversary

I served many customers
during my time at The Diner

Only four of them changed my life
only four of them took a tiny piece of me
that they'll keep forever

Teenagers

Teenagers are
reckless,
impulsive,
selfish

I was never a normal teenager

I never misbehaved,
went out with friends,
got in trouble,
broke curfew,
snuck out

I always felt so grown up at that age

Thinking
I'll never do those things

I'll never misbehave,
get in trouble,
break curfew,
sneak out

And then I met you

It's not that you make me do those things
or that you pressure me
to do those things

It's that you make me want to
misbehave,
break curfew,
sneak out

You make me feel
reckless,
impulsive,
selfish

You make me want to be reckless
to abandon my curfew
to turn off my phone
and drop off the face of the earth with you

You make me feel impulsive
and spontaneous
You make me want to abandon
all of my preconceived ideas
and make new ones

You make me feel selfish
I want to do whatever I want
and not answer to anyone else
I want you all to myself

We're not teenagers anymore
but we are
making up for lost time

We're not teenagers anymore
not in the technical sense
but we still are
in more ways than one

We're not teenagers anymore
we're not inherently
reckless, or
impulsive, or
selfish

We're not teenagers anymore
because we know what we want
we just cannot stand
the obstacles in our way

So let's be teenagers,
just for tonight

Through His Eyes

He sees her with joy
and value

He got to know her as time passed
Her aura
was relaxing
What he didn't know
is that no one had ever described her
as relaxing
Her mother would describe her
as high-strung
neurotic

He would look at her
She seemed shy
at first
and wholesome

She is down-to-earth,
according to him
She has an attitude,
according to others
He sees her
as kind

and thoughtful

As he got to know her
he found
that she is unique,
in the way that
she likes many things
she is unique,
in the way that
she is talented
in many ways

She knows a lot about art
she knows how to work
with many different mediums

He thinks she is remarkable
in the way she expresses herself
through art
and words
He thinks her poems
are very good

The thing about her
that makes his eyes go wide
and makes him drop his jaw
is the way she is so elegant

He can't explain

how she is elegant,
but everytime he focuses on her
His world slows down

When she walks towards him
his world stops
He admires
how gorgeous she is

She's impulsive,
she knows what she wants
and she knows
how to get it

He finds that attractive
it shows her confidence
And helps him understand
she is a strong woman

She's perfect.
Absolutely perfect.

pieces of me

If you think about it,
songs are simply poems
in a different language

Music is simply poetry
in a different key

I listen to music the same way I write:
fully appreciating every lyric,
every strum of the guitar,
every beat of the drums,
admiring the beauty of the singer's voice.
Rewinding to hear it again,
repeating the song over and over,
catching something new with every listen

I write the same way I listen to music:
artfully choosing each word,
every connotation,
every arrangement of letters,
admiring the beauty of the lines
strung together at the end
Rereading the poem over and over,
changing something with every read

The best way to listen to music
is to isolate yourself,
put headphones on,
close your eyes,
and listen

The best way to read a poem
is to isolate yourself,
turn off all the noise,
open your eyes,
and read

These tasks are the same
Slightly different

Singing along to music
is simply
reading poetry aloud,
the artist's voices
intertwined with your own

I wish I could write like a songwriter
Pouring my soul into a song
or an entire album
I wish I could pour my entire soul into a poem
or a book of them

But these poems are just pieces of me

Forever

We say forever
we toss the word around

Forever
What does that mean to you?

When you think of me
What do you picture?

Do you picture us
celebrating our one year anniversary?

Do you picture us
having our first fight,
and not speaking
for the rest of the day?

Do you picture
our first apartment together,
boxes strewn everywhere,
and me painting the kitchen yellow?

Do you picture
the food on the stove burning
and me, on the phone

with the local pizza place,
ordering takeout?

Do you picture
the day my writing lands
on the New York Times bestselling list
and we celebrate together?
Would you pick me up
and spin me around
and kiss me all over?

Do you picture
me getting ready on our wedding day,
with tears in my eyes,
my dress hung up,
waiting to be put on?

Do you picture
coming home from work,
me in the kitchen,
a baby on my hip,
and a screaming toddler in the next room?

I picture this future for us
Forever

9 789357 444200